CONTENTS

WITHDRAWN

Disney

FROZEN

ISBN 978-1-4803-6819-4

WONDERLAND MUSIC COMPANY, INC.

FIVE HUNDRED SOUTH SONGS

DISTRIBUTED BY

HAL•LEONARD®
CORPORATION
7777 W. BLUEMOUND RD. P.O. BOX 13819 MILWAUKEE, WI 53213

In Australia Contact:
Hal Leonard Australia Pty. Ltd.
4 Lentara Court, Cheltenham, Victoria, 3192 Australia
Email: ausadmin@halleonard.com.au

Visit Hal Leonard Online at **www.halleonard.com**

FROZEN HEART

Music and Lyrics by KRISTEN ANDERSON-LOPEZ
and ROBERT LOPEZ

Dirge-like

(Percussion)

Born of cold and win-ter air and moun-tain rain com-bin-ing, ____ this

i-cy force both foul and fair has a fro-zen heart ____ worth ____

min - ing. So, cut! through the heart, cold and clear.

Strike! for __ love and strike for __ fear. See the beau - ty sharp and sheer.

Split the ice __ a - part, __ and break the fro - zen

Faster
D5

heart. Watch your step! Let it go! Rr -

hyup! Ho! Watch your step! Let it go!

Beau - ti - ful! Pow - er - ful! Dan - ger - ous! Cold! Ice has a mag - ic, can't be con - trolled.

Strong - er than one, strong - er than ten, strong - er than a hun - dred men! Hyup!

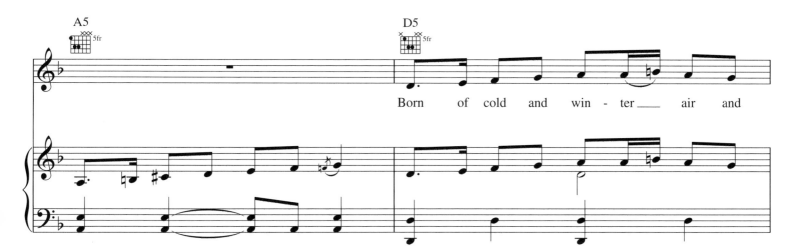

Born of cold and win - ter air and

moun - tain rain com - bin - ing, (this i - cy force both foul and fair has a

DO YOU WANT TO BUILD A SNOWMAN?

Music and Lyrics by KRISTEN ANDERSON-LOPEZ
and ROBERT LOPEZ

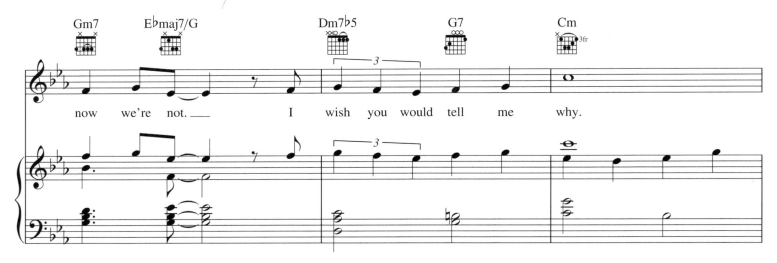

snow - man. **LITTLE ELSA:** *(Spoken:)* Go away, Anna. **LITTLE ANNA:** *(Sung:)* O - kay,

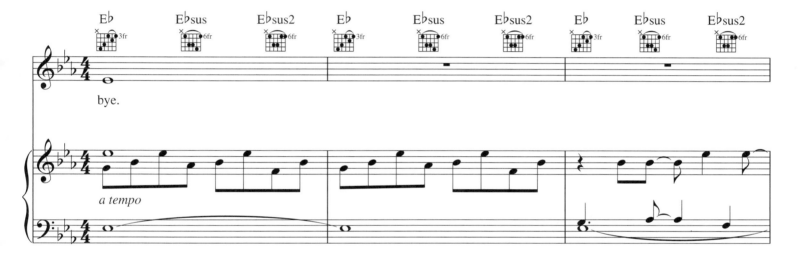

bye.

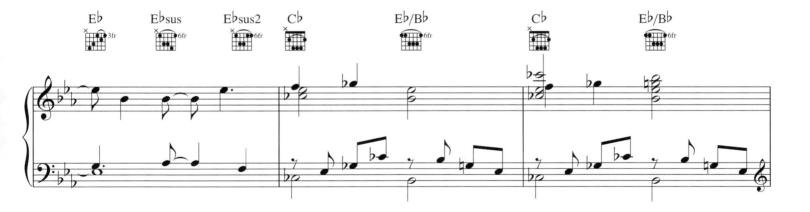

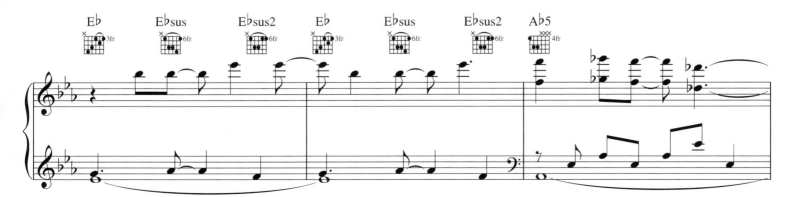

lone - ly, all these emp - ty___ rooms,___ just watch - ing the hours tick

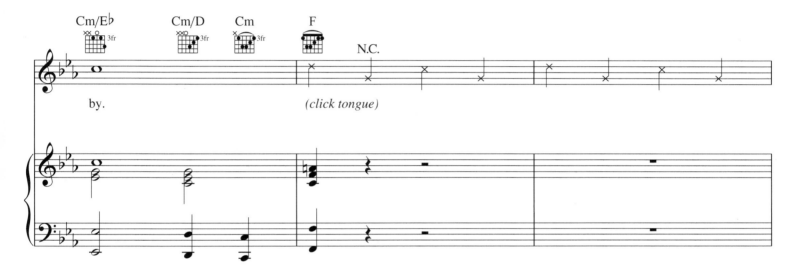

by. *(click tongue)*

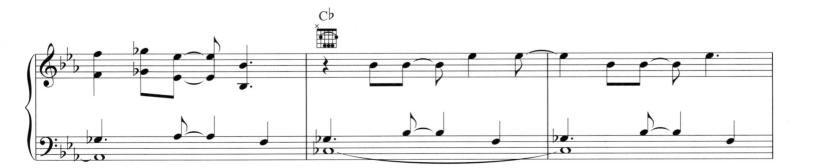

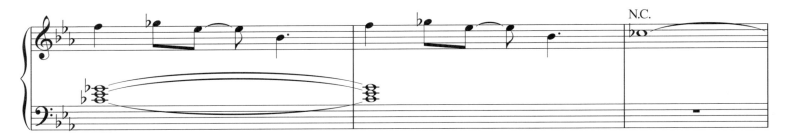

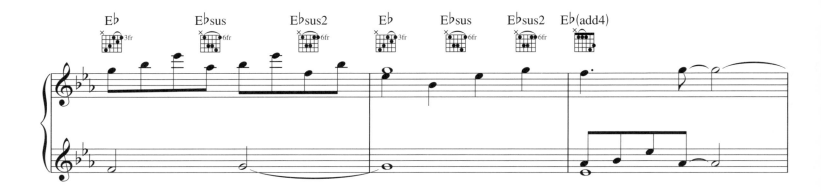

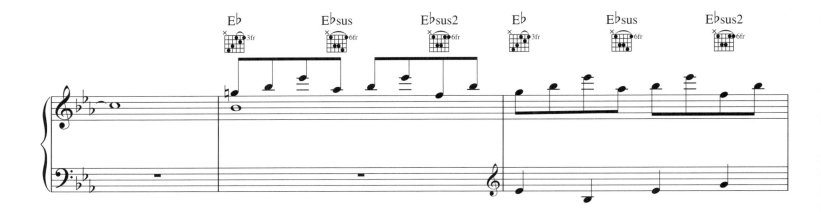

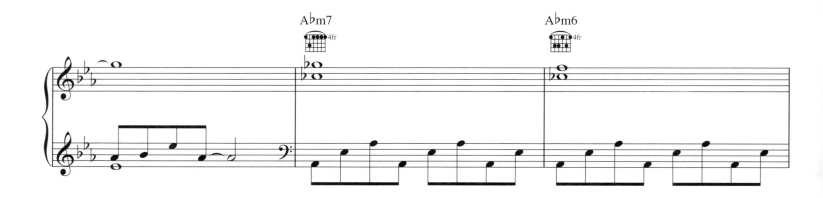

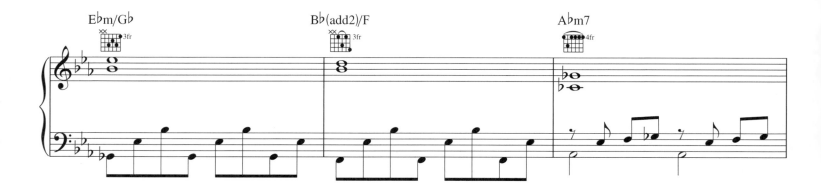

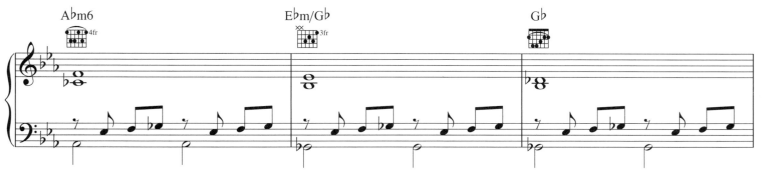

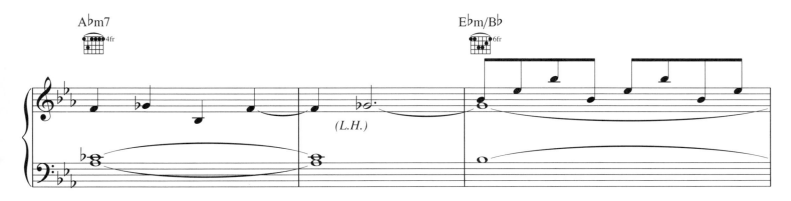

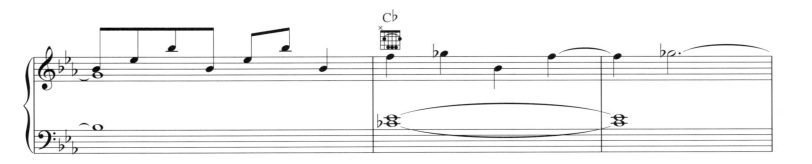

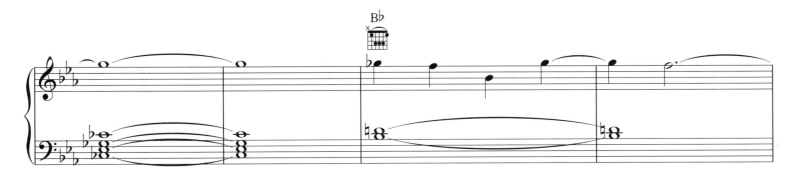

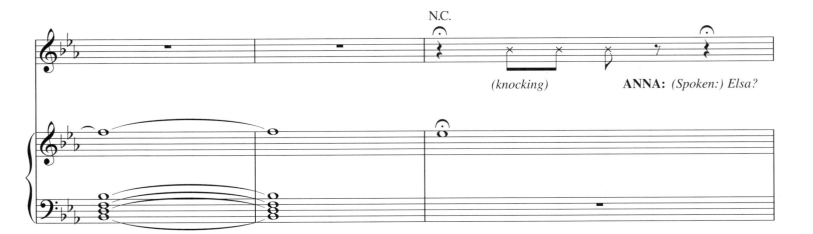

(knocking)   **ANNA:** *(Spoken:) Elsa?*

A little slower, tenderly

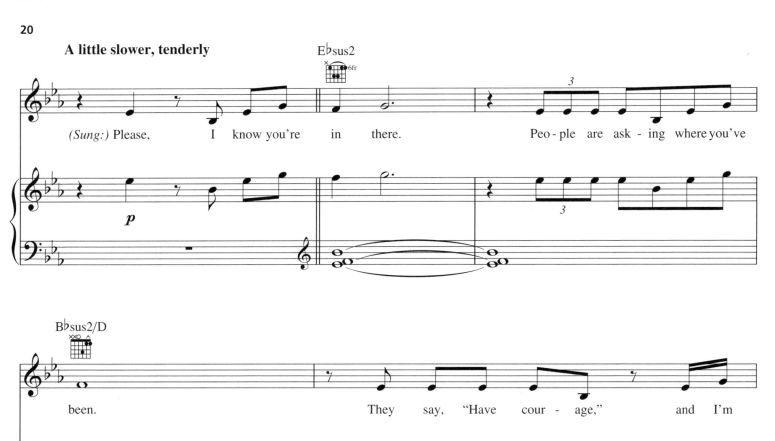

(Sung:) Please, I know you're in there. Peo-ple are ask-ing where you've

been. They say, "Have cour - age," and I'm

try - ing to; I'm right out here for you, just let me in.

We on - ly have each oth - er; it's just you and me. ___

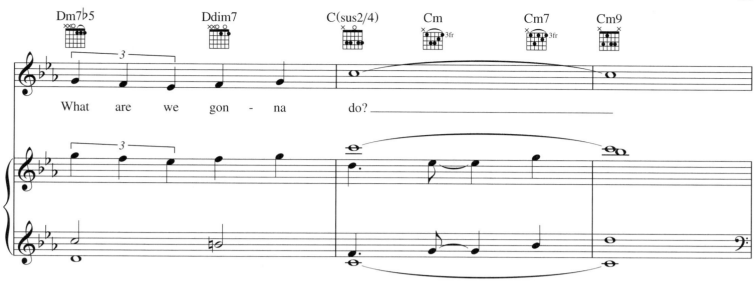

What are we gon - na do? _____

Do you want to build a snow - man?

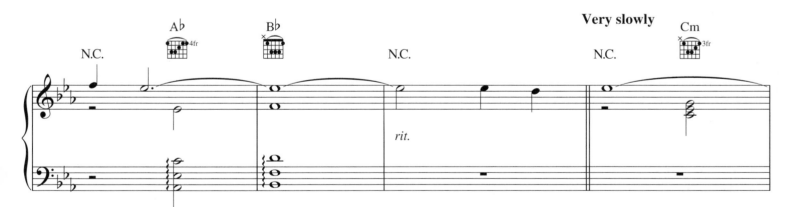

rit.

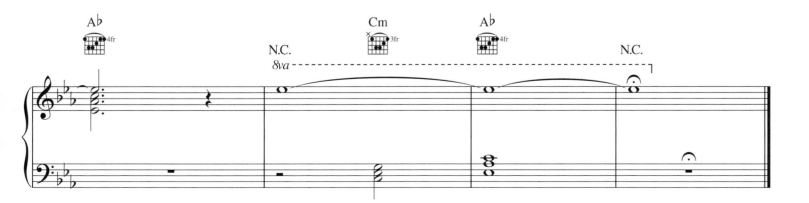

FOR THE FIRST TIME IN FOREVER

Music and Lyrics by KRISTEN ANDERSON-LOPEZ
and ROBERT LOPEZ

ANNA: The win-dow is o-pen! So's_ that door!_ I did-n't know they did that an-y-more._ Who knew we owned_ eight thou-sand sal-ad plates? For years I've roamed_ these emp-ty halls._

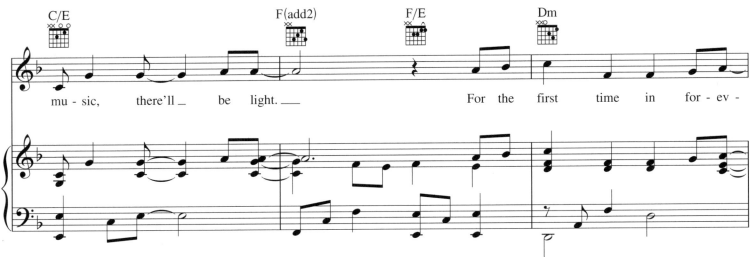

mu - sic, there'll _ be light. _ For the first time in for - ev -

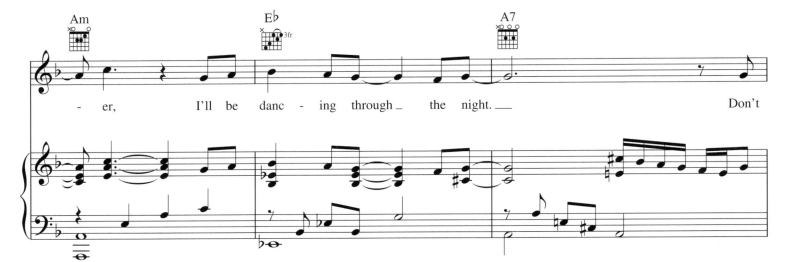

- er, I'll be danc - ing through _ the night. _ Don't

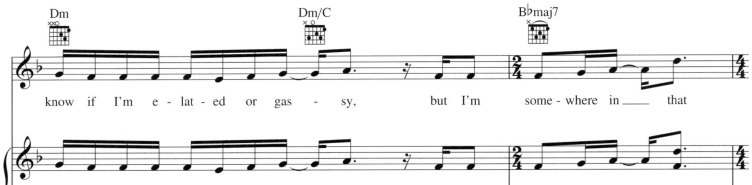

know if I'm e - lat - ed or gas - sy, but I'm some - where in _ that

zone. 'Cause for the first time in for - ev - er, _

Excited again

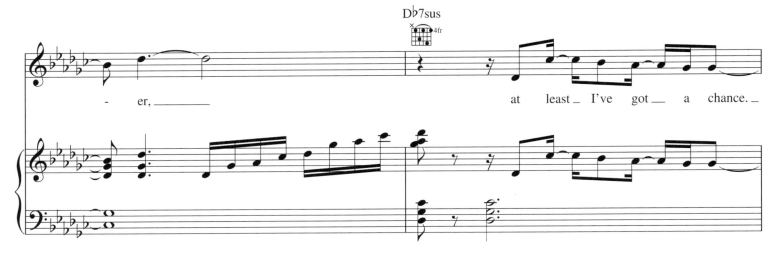

at least __ I've got __ a chance. __

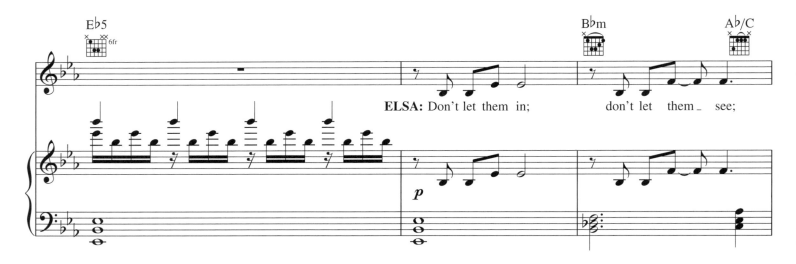

ELSA: Don't let them in; don't let them __ see;

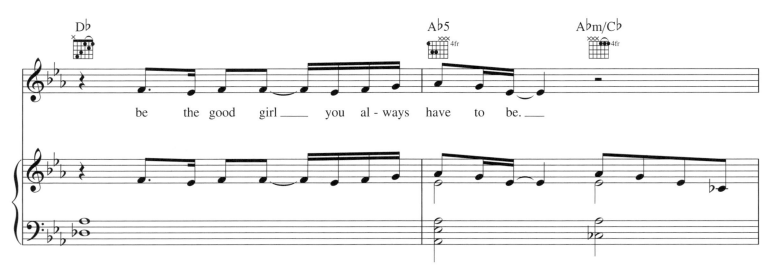

be the good girl __ you al - ways have to be. __

LOVE IS AN OPEN DOOR

Music and Lyrics by KRISTEN ANDERSON-LOPEZ
and ROBERT LOPEZ

HANS: (Spoken:) I was thinking the same thing! 'Cause like, (Sung): I've been search - ing my whole life ___ to find my own place. ___ And may - be it's the par - ty talk - ing, or the cho - c'late fon - due... ___ But with you, _____ but with you, ___ I found my ___

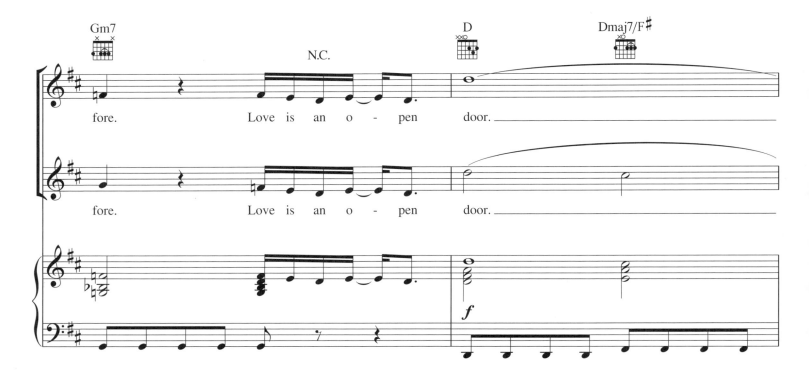

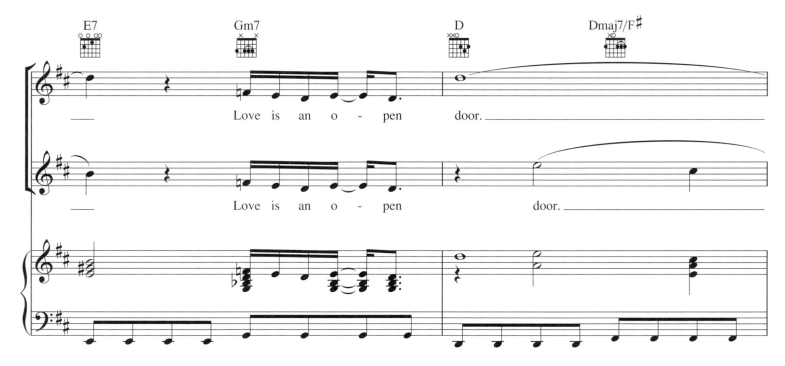

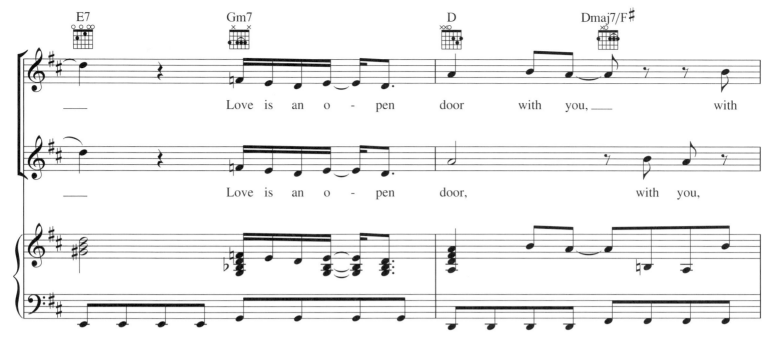

LET IT GO

Music and Lyrics by KRISTEN ANDERSON-LOPEZ
and ROBERT LOPEZ

Half-time feel, mysterious

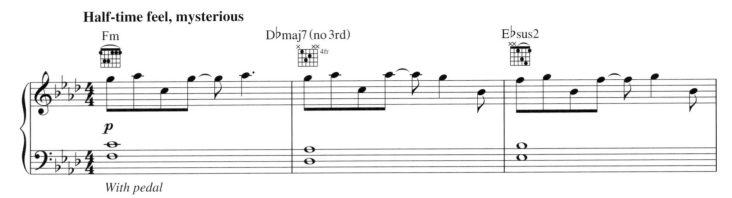

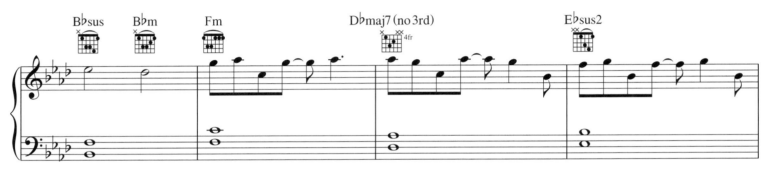

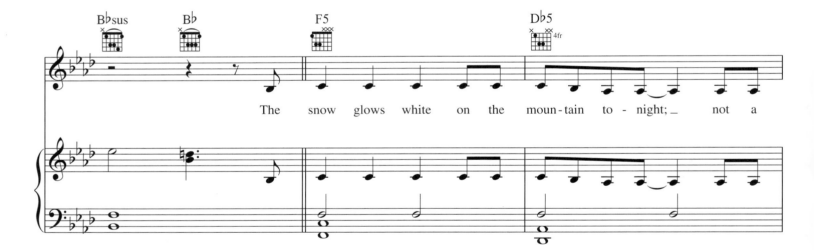

The snow glows white on the moun-tain to-night; — not a

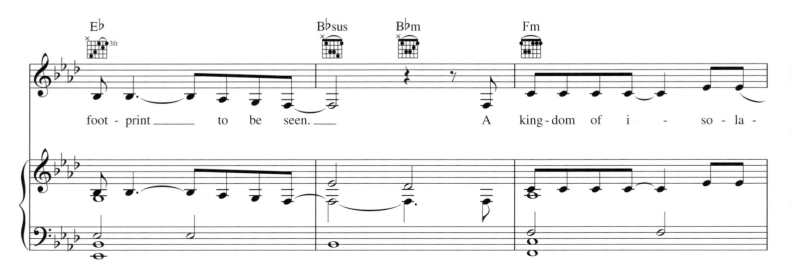

foot-print _____ to be seen. ___ A king-dom of i - so - la-

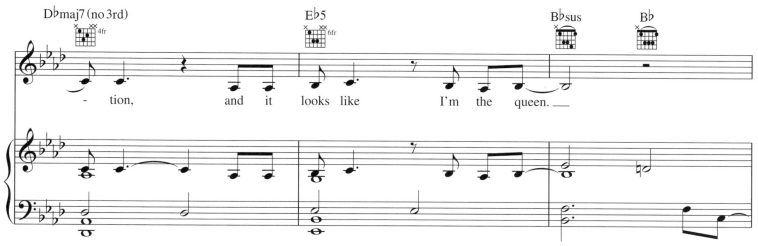

-tion, and it looks like I'm the queen. ___

The wind ___ is howl - ing like ___ this swirl - ing storm ___ in - side. ___

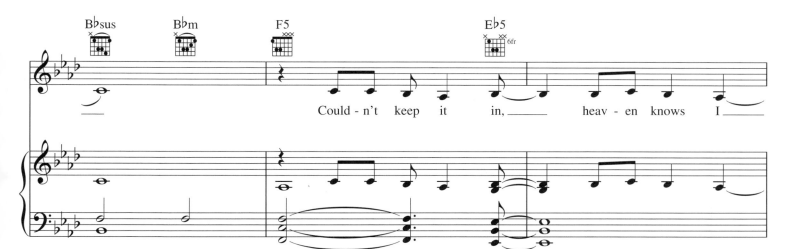

___ Could - n't keep it in, _____ heav - en knows I _____

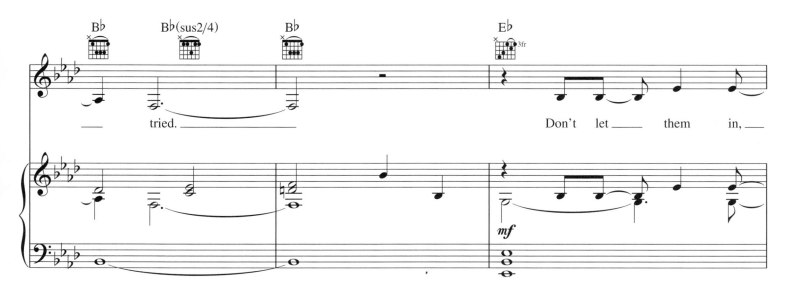

___ tried. _____ Don't let ___ them in, ___

don't let __ them see; be the good girl you al - ways have __ to be.

Con - ceal, __ don't feel, don't let __ them know... _____

Well, now __ they know. _____ Let it go, __

___ let it go; ___ can't __ hold it back an - y - more. __
___ let it go; ___ I am one with the wind and sky. __

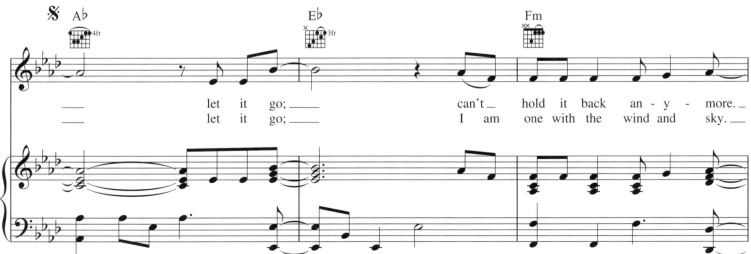

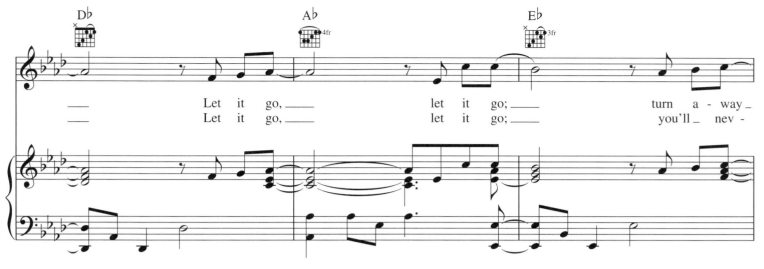

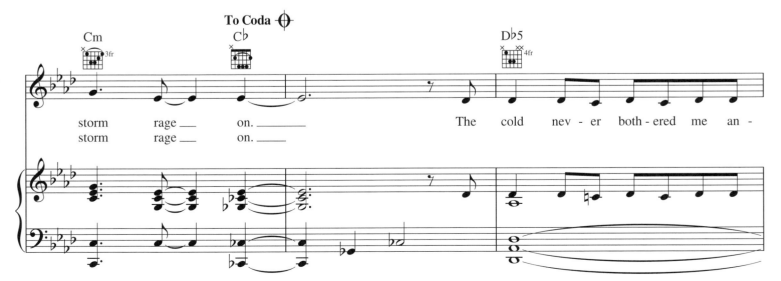

Gaining confidence

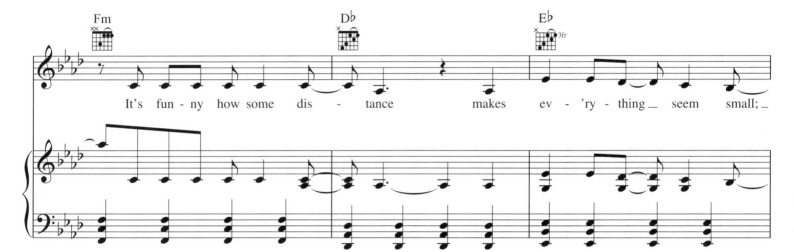

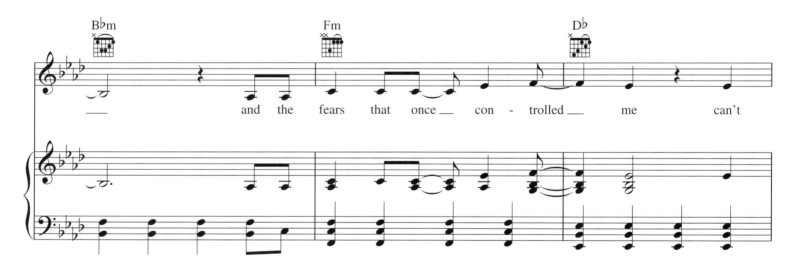

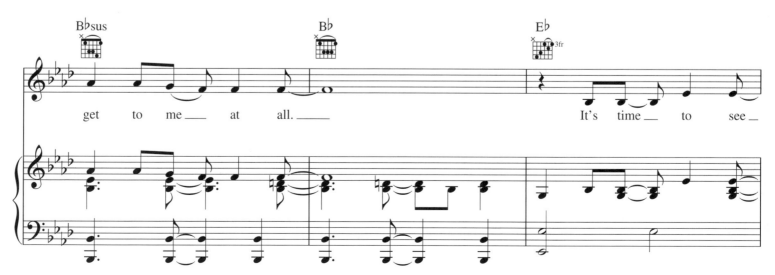

y - way.

It's fun - ny how some dis - tance makes ev - 'ry - thing __ seem small; __

__ and the fears that once __ con - trolled __ me can't

get to me __ at all. __ It's time __ to see __

what I ___ can do, to test ___ the lim - its and ___ break through. ___

No right, ___ no wrong, ___ no rules ___ for me, _____ I'm

D.S. al Coda

CODA

free! _____ Let it go, _

___

My pow - er flur - ries through __ the air __

__ in - to __ the ground. __ My soul __ is spi -

- ral - ing __ in fro - zen frac - tals all __ a - round. __

Eb5

N.C.

And one __ thought cry - stal - li - zes like __ an i - cy blast: __

I'm nev - er go - ing back; _ the

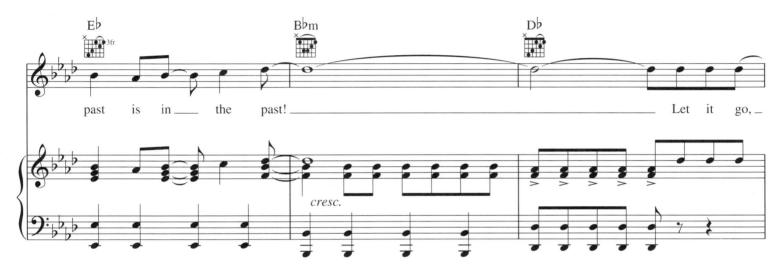

past is in _ the past! _____ Let it go, _

_ let it go, _ and I'll rise _ like the break _ of dawn. _

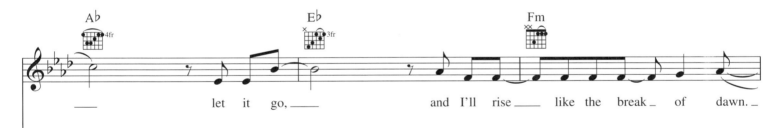

_____ Let it go, _ let it go; _ that per -

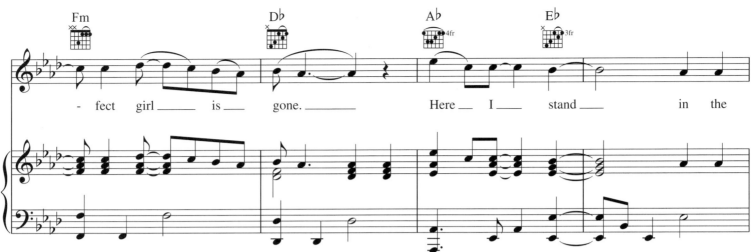

- fect girl _____ is _____ gone. _____ Here _____ I _____ stand _____ in the

light _____ of _____ day; _____ let the

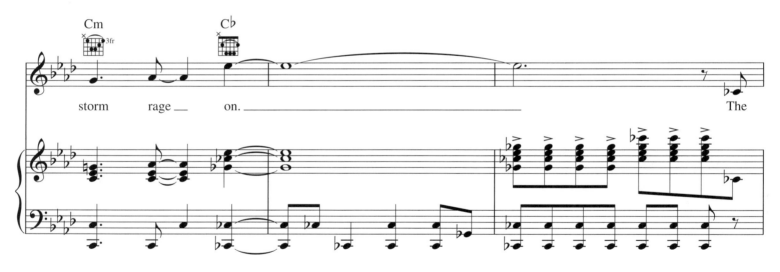

storm rage _____ on. _____ The

cold nev - er both - ered me an - y - way.

REINDEER(S) ARE BETTER THAN PEOPLE

Music and Lyrics by KRISTEN ANDERSON-LOPEZ
and ROBERT LOPEZ

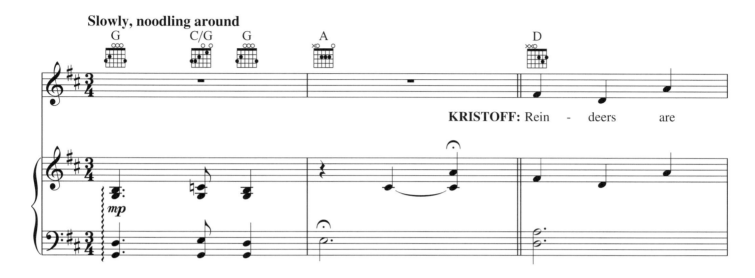

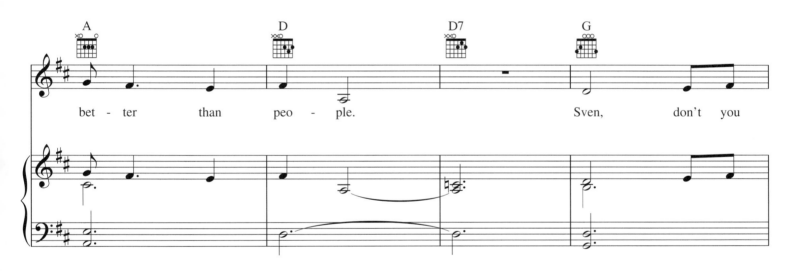

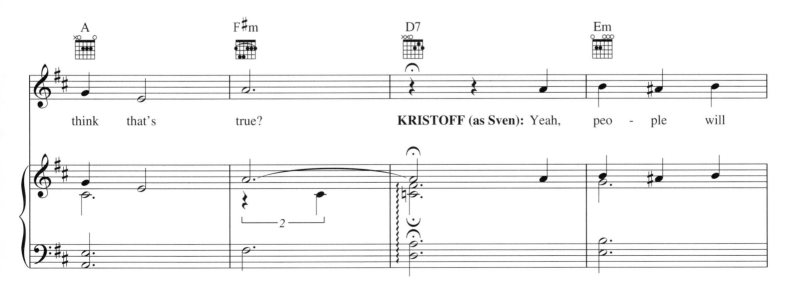

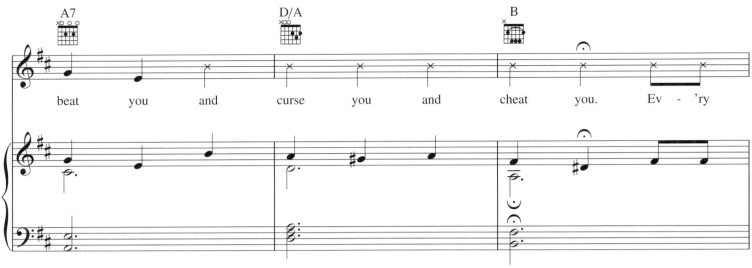

beat you and curse you and cheat you. Ev - 'ry

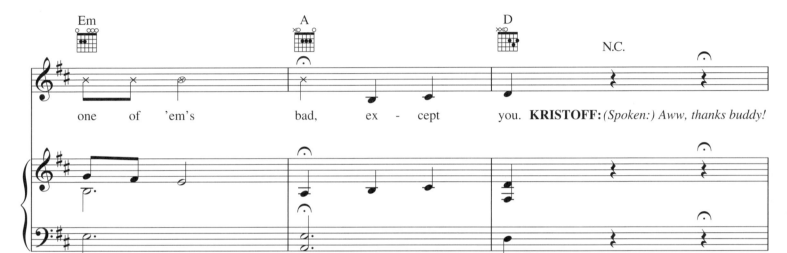

one of 'em's bad, ex - cept you. **KRISTOFF:** *(Spoken:) Aww, thanks buddy!*

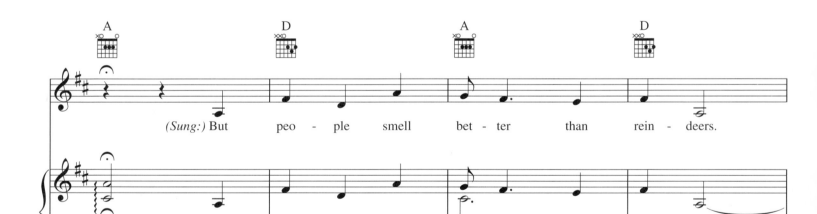

(Sung:) But peo - ple smell bet - ter than rein - deers.

Sven, don't you think I'm right?

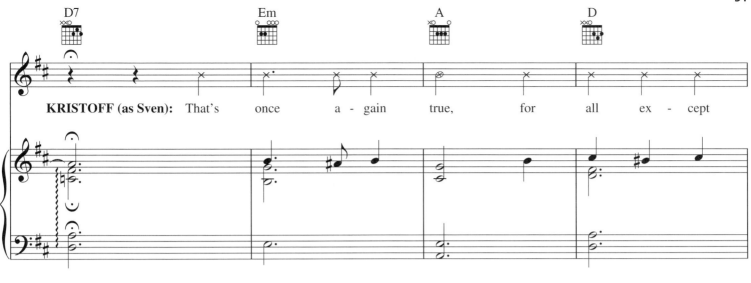

KRISTOFF (as Sven): That's once a - gain true, for all ex - cept

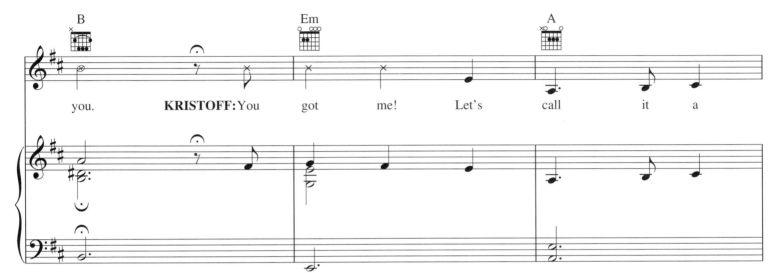

you. KRISTOFF: You got me! Let's call it a

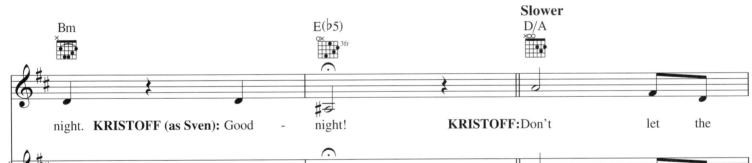

Slower

night. KRISTOFF (as Sven): Good - night! KRISTOFF: Don't let the

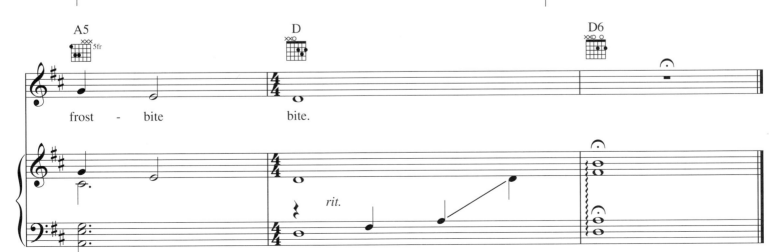

frost - bite bite.

IN SUMMER

Music and Lyrics by KRISTEN ANDERSON-LOPEZ
and ROBERT LOPEZ

Bouncy again

it gets warm.___ And I can't wait to see what my

bud-dies all think of me. Just im-ag-ine how much cool-er I'll be in

sum-mer!_____ Da da, da doo, a

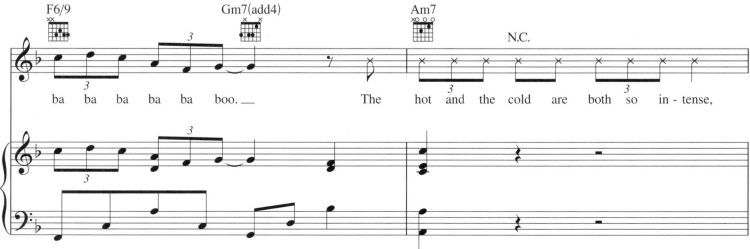

ba ba ba ba ba boo.___ The hot and the cold are both so in-tense,

FOR THE FIRST TIME IN FOREVER (REPRISE)

Music and Lyrics by KRISTEN ANDERSON-LOPEZ
and ROBERT LOPEZ

Moderately

ANNA:
(Spoken:) You don't have to protect me. Please don't shut me out ___ a - gain!
I'm not afraid!

(Sung:) Please don't slam the door. ___ You don't have to keep ___ your dis - tance an - y - more. 'Cause for the first time in for - ev - er, I

change this win-ter weath - er. and ev-'ry-thing will be al -

Ahh... _____ I _____

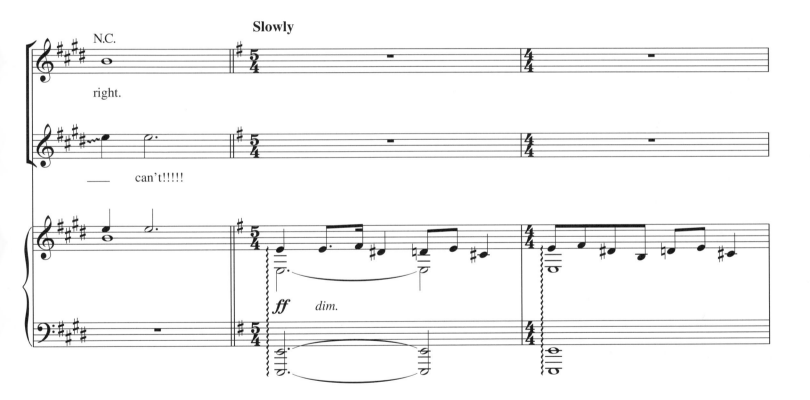

Slowly

N.C.

right.

_____ can't!!!!!

ff *dim.*

FIXER UPPER

Music and Lyrics by KRISTEN ANDERSON-LOPEZ
and ROBERT LOPEZ

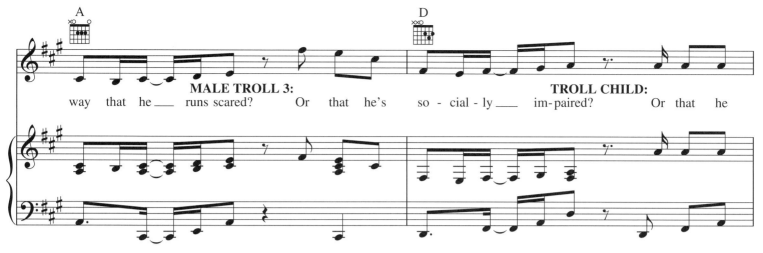

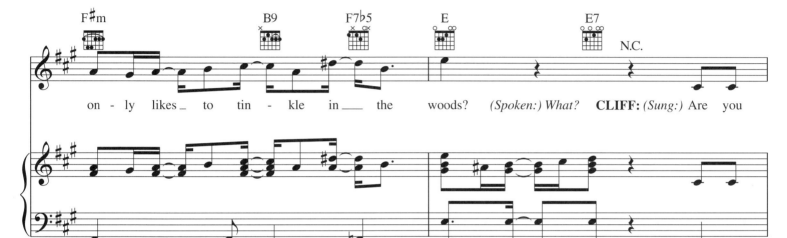

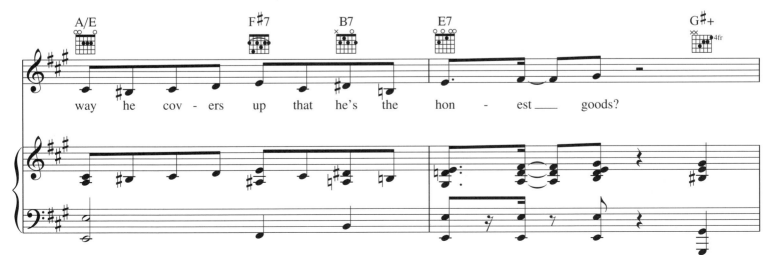

VUELIE

Written by FRODE FJELLHEIM
and CHRISTOPHE BECK

Moderately slow

p

With pedal

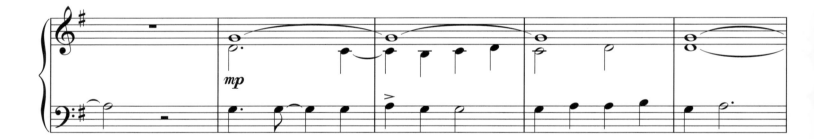

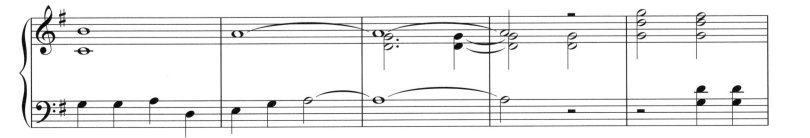

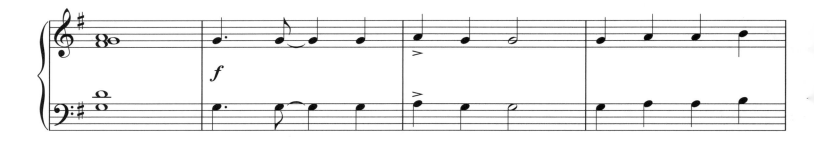

HEIMR ÁRNADALR

Music by CHRISTOPHE BECK
Lyrics by CHRISTINE HALS

Ver-ðug drót-tning stór Hjar-taaf gu-li skín-na
Wer-thoog drawt-ning stor Yar-taf goo-li skeen-na
Wor-thy queen of great-ness the heart of gold shines.__

Kró-num þik með vo-num ást og trú
Crow-noom theek meth vo-num aost og true
We crown you with hope,__ love, and faith.

Fag-ra grýtt-ur land hei-mr Ár-na-dalr Fyl-gið
Fahg-gra grytt-or land hey-mr Are-na-dalr Phyl-gith
Beaut-'ful sto-ney land Home Aren-delle__ Fol-low

drótt - nin - gu ljó - sins
drawt - nin - goo ljo - since
queen _ (of) light. _

drótt - nin - gu
drawt - nin - goo
Queen _ (of)

Fyl - gið ljó - sins Ver - ðug
Phyl - gith ljo - since Wer - thoog
fol - low the light wor - thy

drót - tning stór
drawt - ning stor
queen of great - ness

Várr
Vaorr
Our

drot - tning
drawt - ning
queen _

Ver - ðug
Wer - thøog
wor - thy

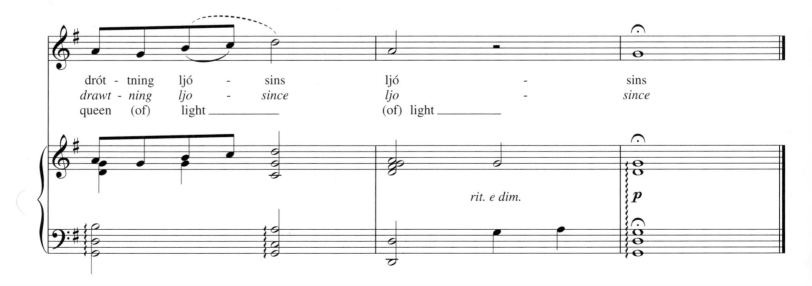

drót - tning ljó - sins
drawt - ning ljo - since
queen (of) light _____

ljó - sins
ljo - since
(of) light _____

rit. e dim.

p